STEM IN THE SUMMER OLYMPICS

THE SCIENCE BEHIND
CYCLING

by Jenny Fretland VanVoorst

Ideas for Parents and Teachers

Pogo Books let children practice reading informational text while introducing them to nonfiction features such as headings, labels, sidebars, maps, and diagrams, as well as a table of contents, glossary, and index.

Carefully leveled text with a strong photo match offers early fluent readers the support they need to succeed.

Before Reading

- "Walk" through the book and point out the various nonfiction features. Ask the student what purpose each feature serves.
- Look at the glossary together. Read and discuss the words.

Read the Book

- Have the child read the book independently.
- Invite him or her to list questions that arise from reading.

After Reading

- Discuss the child's questions. Talk about how he or she might find answers to those questions.
- Prompt the child to think more. Ask: Olympic cyclists use their skills to bike fast! How could you bike faster?

Pogo Books are published by Jump!
5357 Penn Avenue South
Minneapolis, MN 55419
www.jumplibrary.com

Library of Congress Cataloging-in-Publication Data

Names: Fretland VanVoorst, Jenny, 1972- author.
Title: The science behind cycling / by Jenny Fretland VanVoorst.
Description: Minneapolis, Minnesota: Jump!, Inc., 2020.
Series: STEM in the Summer Olympics
Includes bibliographical references and index.
Audience: Age 7 to 10.
Identifiers: LCCN 2018058168 (print)
LCCN 2018059996 (ebook)
ISBN 9781641289047 (ebook)
ISBN 9781641289023 (hardcover: alk. paper)
Subjects: LCSH: Cycling—Juvenile literature.
Sports sciences—Juvenile literature.
Classification: LCC GV1043.5 (ebook)
LCC GV1043.5 .F74 2020 (print) | DDC 796.6/2—dc23
LC record available at https://lccn.loc.gov/2018058168

Editor: Susanne Bushman
Designer: Michelle Sonnek

Photo Credits: Valeri Potapova/Shutterstock, cover (clipboard); Serdar Tibet/Shutterstock, cover (helmet); Tim de Waele/Getty, 1, 5, 6t, 6b, 8, 15, 16-17, 18-19; stockphoto-graf/Shutterstock, 3; MAHATHIR MOHD YASIN/Shutterstock, 4; Eric Feferberg/AFP/Getty, 6-7t, 12-13; Foto Arena LTDA/Alamy, 6-7b; Peter De Voecht/Photonews/Getty, 9; Petr Toman/Shutterstock, 10-11; Sergiy Zavgorodny/Shutterstock, 14; dpa picture alliance/Alamy, 20-21; Nungning20/Shutterstock, 23.

Printed in the United States of America at Corporate Graphics in North Mankato, Minnesota.

TABLE OF CONTENTS

CHAPTER 1

GOING FOR GOLD

Do you like to ride your bike? Would you like to be a professional cyclist?

gold
medal

These athletes take cycling to the next level. They use science to be the best. They use high-tech **equipment**. They train hard. And they compete for Olympic gold!

road cycling

track cycling

BMX cycling

mountain biking

There are four Olympic cycling events. What are they? Road cycling. Track cycling. BMX cycling. Mountain biking. Each requires a special bike. Athletes use different skills, too.

CHAPTER 2

BIKES AND TIRES

Olympic cycling is all about going fast. How do cyclists create speed? Power! Good equipment helps, too.

Bicycle frames are light. Why?
They require less **energy** to move.
But they are still strong and sturdy.

Bike tires rub against the ground. This creates **friction**. It slows the bike down. Tires are built to avoid this.

Mountain bike and BMX tires are soft. They don't press into loose or rocky soil. This creates less friction. They are also thick and knobby. Why? They have better **traction**.

DID YOU KNOW?

Wheels are strong. They can support 400 times their own weight!

disc wheel

Tires on road and track bikes are firm. Why? They do not flatten much. They are thinner, too. Why? Less tire touches the ground. This creates less friction. What does that mean? More speed!

Most bikes have **spokes**. Not track bikes! Some have solid disc wheels. Air flows smoothly around the discs. This reduces **drag**.

TAKE A LOOK!

Each cycle has unique tires. Compare their features.

BMX CYCLING

Thick, knobby tires handle better. They are small and light. This allows for quick **acceleration**.

MOUNTAIN BIKING

Thick, knobby, and soft tires allow for better traction.

ROAD CYCLING

Smooth, thin, and firm tires lessen friction.

TRACK CYCLING

Disc wheels lessen drag.

CHAPTER 3

RACE TIME!

A cyclist can also cause drag. How? Air catches on a cyclist's body or loose clothing. Drag slows the cyclist down.

Olympic cyclists dress to reduce drag. Tight clothing and **streamlined** helmets help. There is no extra material to create drag.

velodrome

Track cyclists race in a **velodrome**. It has raised ends. The oval shape creates a **centripetal force**. How? It pushes riders inward. It keeps them from biking off the track at curves!

DID YOU KNOW?

In some track events, many racers **jostle** for position. In these events, only back wheels have discs. Why? So athletes have more control of their bikes.

Air is pushed aside as cyclists ride. This means there is no wind directly behind them. Other riders bike there. This is called **drafting**.

These riders can use less energy. How much less? Up to 40 percent. The riders can use the energy later. When? For a burst of speed near the finish line!

DID YOU KNOW?

Some bikes have curved handlebars. The rider leans low over them. His or her body makes a rounded shape. Air flows over the rider's back.

drafting

There is a lot of science behind cycling. Wind tunnels help study riding positions. **Engineers** also test new materials. They want to create lighter, stronger bikes.

Olympic cyclists pedal hard. They use physics and science to win big!

Va: 30,1 km/h
T: 22,3 °C
Beta: 0,0 Grad

wind tunnel

ACTIVITIES & TOOLS

TREAD TEST

Your shoes are like tires for your feet! Explore how the material and tread pattern of your shoe soles affects traction on different surfaces.

What You Need:
- Several different shoes, such as sneakers, dress shoes, and sandals.
- A variety of surfaces, such as tile, linoleum, carpet, grass, and dirt.

1 **Make a chart comparing shoe against surface, like this:**

	tile	linoleum	carpet	grass	dirt
sneakers					
dress shoes					
sandals					

2 **Try on each pair of shoes and experiment by walking, running, and sliding across each surface. Be careful! Did you stick or slide? Record your traction on each surface.**

3 **Look at your data. Which shoes slipped the most on which surfaces? Which shoes provided the best traction?**

4 **Now consider what each kind of shoe is designed for. Does the amount of traction the shoe provides match its use?**

5 **What shoe features do you think help most with traction? Is it the tread patterns? Is it the sole material?**

6 **Finally, consider why different types of shoes might need different treads.**

acceleration: An increase in speed.

centripetal force: The force that acts in a direction toward a center or axis.

drafting: The practice of riding closely behind another cyclist in the windless area he or she creates.

drag: The force that slows or blocks motion or advancement.

energy: The ability or strength to do things without getting tired.

engineers: People who design systems, structures, products, or machines.

equipment: The tools and products needed for specific purposes, such as athletic events.

friction: The force that slows down objects when they rub against each other.

jostle: To come in close contact with other people or objects.

spokes: The thin rods that connect the rim of a wheel to the hub.

streamlined: Designed or shaped to reduce the resistance to air or water.

traction: The force that keeps a moving body from slipping on a surface.

velodrome: An oval course with elevated ends on which Olympic track cyclists compete.

INDEX

TO LEARN MORE

Finding more information is as easy as 1, 2, 3.

1. Go to www.factsurfer.com
2. Enter "sciencebehindcycling" into the search box.
3. Choose your book to see a list of websites.

FACT SURFER